Seven C's to Calm

Reclaiming your anxiety-free self

By

Caroline C Cunningham

A CIP catalogue record for this title is available from
the British Library.

Note:

The information in the 'Seven C's to Calm' booklet
should not be considered as a replacement for
professional medical treatment: a physician should
be consulted in all matters relating to health and
especially in relation to any symptoms which may
require diagnosis or medical attention. While the
advice and information in this book are given based
on the author's experience, life studies and personal
observation, neither the author nor the publisher can
accept any legal responsibility for any injury
sustained whilst following any of the suggestions
made herein.

Foreword:

Anxiety (including panic attacks) can have such a negative impact in our lives and can prevent us from reaching our true potential.

As someone who has been (and continues to be) determined to move beyond the limits of anxiety, I'd like to share what I have learned with you.

In this short book-let, I do not dwell on the wide range of unpleasant (and sometimes frightening) sensations and tensions associated with anxiety. I'm assuming you are well acquainted with those sensations and are eager to free yourself since you have chosen to join me here.

This simple guide '**Seven C's to Calm – Reclaiming your anxiety-free self'** has been created to prepare you for your journey towards a calmer and more capable you.

There is so much information available to us in these times. Books, blogs, videos and a variety of internet media platforms offer a plenitude of resources for learning about many topics including anxiety.

However, it can often be confusing as to where to start and not every voice is the one that we can hear effectively.

I am passionate about authenticity and well-being and have seen for myself that the two are truly linked.

I also believe that it is never too late for someone to make a start on their road to recovery. The practice of learning and adapting is simply required.

External support (therapy), can also be very beneficial for keeping on track. Be assured, a place of calm exists within you, it's just a matter of finding your way.

It is my sincere wish that this short guide will help you to get started on your path to calm and authenticity. You deserve to have the best possible experience in this wonderful lifetime!

While reading **'Seven C's to Calm – Reclaiming your anxiety-free self'** I recommend you have a dedicated notebook which you will find useful for some of the exercises herein.

Alternatively, a short work-book at the end of this booklet is provided to get you started with your notes and reminders.

Here's to your success in reclaiming your anxiety-free self!

About The Author:

Caroline Cunningham originally graduated with a Degree in Science, a Graduate Diploma in Toxicology and a Higher Diploma in Education in the early 1990's.

Previously a teacher of Maths, Science and presenter of Astronomy, Caroline has later emerged as a visual artist, writer, story-teller, holistic therapist and founder of Authentic Reflexology.

Caroline's journey to authenticity started in earnest in 1999. It was at this time that she created the image 'Break True' which marked a significant turning point in her life.

As a result of extensive studies at 'Bel Canto School of Singing' (Dublin, Ireland) it became apparent to Caroline that we all have unique talents to share and by digging deeper we truly discover our own strengths and gifts.

In 2017, Caroline published her first book of poetry entitled 'The Whisperings of Nature' intended as a source of wisdom, comfort and inspiration.

Caroline also writes and mentors on topics of Authentic Path (personal journey), health & well-being, and art. Her paintings are colourful and call our attention to the beauty inherent in Nature, people and places.

Caroline is the founder of 'Authentic Reflexology' holistic therapy, through which she provides treatment to her clients and encourages self-care.

To find out more about Caroline Cunningham's work visit www.carolinecunningham.com

Break True – Artist Caroline Cunningham

The Seven C's   **Page**

Butterfly in the Lavendar

1. COMFORT

Often we ignore the signs and symptoms of our anxiety until things get to a critical point where we have no choice but to acknowledge that something is wrong. In such moments, we are forced to stop and look at what has happened.

Before we examine the components of anxiety, in an attempt to comprehend what is actually happening, I recommend that you bring yourself into a place of comfort because that is exactly what is needed when our anxiety has completely arrested us.

What can you do in this moment, or in this day to experience comfort, if even for five minutes? My favourites are time spent in Nature, particularly amongst trees.

Other suggestions include spending a few minutes reading words of wisdom and inspiration, engaging with holistic therapy or listening to soothing music. What about noticing the beautiful colours of flowers or surrounding yourself with uplifting aromas of carefully selected essential oils?

Notice I am not referring to food, alcohol or other activities that can be associated with addictive tendencies that serve to mask our discomfort.

Think about the simple things that allow for comfort and start by giving yourself this experience. Why not make a list right now of those things that you feel will give you comfort in this very moment?

Be gentle with yourself. The worst has not yet happened. How do I know? Because your anxiety is constantly creating a more fantastically disastrous outcome!

No matter what happens in the future, we are forced to accept that so much is out of our control. That is why it is so important to feel good in the present moment.

By cultivating this state of comfort and calm you will be more prepared for all outcomes.

A little mantra that I found useful in the past:

'I am cool, calm, clear, collected'

Perhaps you will find this a useful phrase to meditate on as you rest in your place of comfort.

2. COMPREHEND

A very important teacher in my life instilled the message that calm and relaxation are by-products of knowledge.

In other words, when we concentrate on learning the facts and knowing the origins of our chosen topic we can bring more command and calm to what we do. This is also true of knowing ourselves more fully.

You may have heard the expression 'safe in the knowledge that...'

Let's be safe in the knowledge that we know what is happening in those moments of anxiety.

- What is anxiety?
- What are your anxiety symptoms?
- What is happening inside your body when you experience anxiety?

These are questions I urge you to investigate and find the answers to.

There is a reason why I am not providing this information fully here:

We learn in a much more powerful and lasting way when we take action and responsibility for our learning

To test this out, I am setting an additional exercise for you. By visiting the book section of my website and clicking on the 'book blog' area, you will find additional articles relating to the topic of anxiety and calm.

I want you to be 'safe in the knowledge' that you know how others currently define the term 'anxiety' and see if it fits your own definition.

My personal definition of anxiety is:

'thoughts and concerns about my future that give rise to great unease and discomfort, which in turn, can prevent me from taking action to have more positive experience and outcomes than those imagined.'

What's your definition, have you checked the dictionaries first?

My personal symptoms of anxiety have been:

tension in a particular area of my body, shallow breathing, a disconnected feeling, feeling that I'm going to lose control and lose consciousness or fall off something (in times of panic/anxiety attack).

Anxiety symptoms vary from person to person they are not in themselves life threatening, but long-term effects are not good for your overall health and can have more serious impact later on.

If you are uncertain or worried about your symptoms it is wise to have a medical professional make an assessment.

Anxiety and panic symptoms can range from palpitations, shortness of breath or shallow breathing, tension, dizziness, uneasy tummy, sweating, unsteady or trembling feeling, apprehension or fear.

When allowed to go unchallenged these uncomfortable sensations can cause a person to avoid certain situations e.g. socialising or leaving their home which in turn can limit their ability to experience all that life can offer. Further distress such as loneliness and depression can often result.

Take time to notice the symptoms you are experiencing. Do you have these symptoms all the time or only in certain situations?

Take a week or two to monitor these symptoms and their intensities. Put yourself in the position of an observer or reporter for this exercise. Refrain from judging yourself harshly. Resist the urge to be annoyed or overwhelmed by what you notice. Remain gentle in your observations.

Is there a common theme to your anxiety? What is the main fixation of your anxiety or the situation in which you feel most impacted? These are the clues to resolving your anxiety completely. For now we are focussed on the baby steps towards restoring and reclaiming calm.

Now take time to research the physiological processes that are at play inside your body when anxiety is at large.

You will learn about hormones that impact other hormones preparing you for 'fight or flight'.

You may learn about the effects of shortness of breath and how it affects the nourishment of the cells in your entire body.

You may learn about the effects that all this 'extra work' of being tense and anxious has on your bodies energy level and your sleep pattern, which in turn have further negative impact on your ability to concentrate and think clearly.

If you are truly interested in letting go of anxiety, I urge you to make the effort to comprehend and be safe in the knowledge that you really know what is going on!

You will find articles covering the physiological aspects of anxiety on my website www.carolinecunningham.com perhaps this can be the start of your 'active' investigation hence making your knowledge stronger.

3. CHALLENGE

Give yourself credit for reading this far, you are already taking up the challenge. You have shown curiosity and are preparing for the next step. You may find resistance to what I am about to tell you next.

You are the only person who can successfully relieve your anxiety!

When anxiety is severe, medical intervention is one of the options available to quell the debilitating effects. Your medical doctor should know your history and disposition in order to assess if this is the best course of action for you.

Bear in mind that medication does not resolve the *cause* of anxiety; it simply alters the chemistry of the body to relieve discomfort.

Medications usually have their own side-effects so be fully informed of these too. Your doctor may prescribe short-term medication combined with a natural therapy, in order to resolve your anxiety more successfully.

The decision of which route to take to reclaiming your anxiety-free self, remains completely your own.

Here, I simply offer some alternative solutions, if even to give a picture of what it looks like to work towards a feeling of empowerment.

Take responsibility for your actions. Life is precious and relatively short. I urge you to make the most of it. Your presence in this world is as important and necessary as that of any other living being.

You may not feel this way now but part of your challenge is to discover that which is truly special about you. In your place of comfort remember this is so and be open to receiving that acknowledgment in your heart.

Are you ready to make a difference to how you experience life?

Do you prefer things as they are?

Do you want to make a positive change?

Are you still curious about this journey to a calmer version of yourself?

Let's go!

4. COMMIT

Your next task is to make a clear commitment on your journey towards calm. Make a three month plan. Change may happen slowly so you may not notice the effects at first.

If you make a daily commitment over at least three months this is a decent length of time in which you should notice significant change.

Make a daily and weekly commitment. Outline the things you are going to do in each of these time frames.

From previous stages you have identified and listed your own personal anxiety feelings and the situations in which you experience these the most.

For starters, pick just one of these symptoms and a situation in which you feel most tense. Allocate a score from 1 to 5 as to the intensity with which you have experienced discomfort in most recent times.

For example: 1 representing barely noticeable symptoms and 5 being the most intensely you have ever experienced anxiety symptoms.

What is your overall goal?

Make a statement about what you would like to achieve from this exercise.

For example: *I want to experience more calm when I am in situations where I am meeting new people or I want to experience calm when I am making a presentation.*

Maybe your anxiety is related to a specific phobia or a traumatic experience from your past. Identify a significant goal that would count as a result for you. Write it down!

Make a list of things you are going to do, on a daily and weekly basis for the next three months, that will bring a sense of calm to your life.

Remember, this is about small steps. If you want to climb the highest mountain and see the best views ever, you must prepare by trekking in its foothills and those closer to your door. Give yourself a challenge that you feel is achievable but also demands some effort on your part.

Suggestions for your daily plan include:

- Return to your place of comfort once a day or ideally three times a day.

- Practice mindful and slow deep breathing exercises allowing your tummy to expand as you breath in through your nose and letting go of tension as you breath out through your mouth.

- Eat nutritious food and reduce your intake of stimulants such as alcohol, and caffeine.

- Keep your body hydrated with plenty of water

- Stretch your body especially after being seated for long periods.

- Exercise daily or at least a few times a week and get plenty of fresh air where possible

- Carry something with you that reminds you of your commitment to calm e.g. a smooth stone or crystal, a small book of comforting phrases, an inspiring image or phrase

- Listening to calming music or a meditation, especially before sleeping.

- Use of specially chosen aromatherapy oils which can have a calming effect e.g. Lavender, Bergamot, Rose, Ylang Ylang, Frankincense and Chamomile

- Check-in to how you are feeling and record your symptom score as suggested here

Suggestions for your weekly plan:

- Learning about your specific anxiety by reading articles and recommended books. I highly recommend Dr. Áine Tubridy's book *'When Panic Attacks'* for those who are experiencing panic/anxiety attacks.

- Seeking expert help with the view to breaking the habit of being tense or to disrupt excessive or out-of-control thought patterns. Choose a therapy that is right for you and a therapist who has the most experience in dealing with your particular concern. It is best to get a recommendation and check too if your therapist is listed within their regulating body or group.

  My preferences have been for reflexology, aromatherapy massage and hypnotherapy. I have engaged with a wide range of therapies in the past, they all have something to offer and can be appropriate to your needs at different times for example, talking therapy may be useful if you have never expressed your feelings before and don't know how. You will know very quickly what is right for you.

- Reviewing your week. What were you particularly pleased about or what would you like to improve next time? Remember to be gentle with yourself. Refrain from feeling that this it too difficult. You are making an effort; that counts for something!

Give yourself a chance to succeed. Change is such a mental challenge for us all and requires a strong positive attitude. You can do this!

This is your challenge, your responsibility, your choice. You get to decide the rules and guidelines for your strategy for restoring calm.

Don't make it about overcoming an obstacle; rather think about how much calm you want to experience.

Hold on to that feeling, relish it and make it real!

5. CHECK-IN

Are you ready for the present? The present is what you are experiencing right now. If you are using social media you cannot escape the messages that are constantly shared to remind us of the importance of being in the present moment.

Make every part of your day count and make a decision to 'check-in' to how you are feeling on a regular basis. Use your scoring guide from the previous section to help monitor your progress.

If you are not sure about how you are feeling, then give yourself a positive suggestion. 'I love myself!' you can't get a more positive feeling than that. If you feel at odds with saying this maybe you can introduce it to your challenge so that in three months time you will feel much more at ease with making that statement.

Another check-in activity which has great benefits is to make a mental list on a daily basis of the things for which you are most grateful. It is a useful to do this especially at the close of our day.

What about reminding yourself on a daily basis, of the things which you really like about yourself or the achievements that you are most proud of?

Maybe you made a difference to someone else's life, maybe you demonstrated a skill that you have learned or a talent that you nurtured and improved? Maybe you experienced a day free from anxiety?

Keep checking in, keep positive and stay on track with your plan.

6. CONQUER

Nothing worthwhile was ever achieved without taking action of some sort. It takes courage to conquer your fears or to move beyond your comfort zone.

Have you heard the saying that 'there is comfort in discomfort?' It's easier to stay within the confines of what we are familiar with. Even if it our experience is very uncomfortable, we may fear the unknown much more.

Staying in that confined place has its own dangers however. You may be missing out on some basic human needs such as the intimacy of relationships or maybe your sense of self-worth is suffering because you have not dared to develop your strengths and talents.

Neglecting your basic needs can also lead to loneliness, low self-esteem and depression, so it is important to take good care of yourself.

Think of the word 'conquer', think of the energy you associate with that word. Does it feel powerful? Can you feel the sense of action attached to this word?

Create a mental image of a person who has 'conquered' or about to 'conquer' something. Does the word 'warrior' come to mind? Or maybe you see a mountaineering/athletic type of person.

Maybe you have a particular real life hero in mind, someone who has already inspired you by that which they have conquered. This could also be somebody who has coped with a life threatening illness or disability in a most positive and inspiring way.

Put yourself in the shoes of the conqueror. Feel the energy that you associate with conquering and achievement. Using the imagination is a powerful way to alter the biochemistry of our body and has the capacity to change how we feel.

Remember you are also somebody who is capable of inspiring others. You are about to make a commitment to conquering your own anxiety. You are about to restore that wonderful feeling of calm that is exists within you.

7. CELEBRATE

On every step of your journey towards calm I encourage you to celebrate. I associate celebration with joy. You don't know if tomorrow will be yours so make the most of 'now' by celebrating (even just silently) your achievements.

I am celebrating the fact that I have written this book-let on your behalf. I am celebrating the fact that my personal experiences of anxiety and panic attacks are serving the purpose of helping others.

Always celebrate your achievements especially as they are often hard won. When you get to your three month review make sure to celebrate in a significant way. Give yourself a well deserved vacation or a special treat or gift. You could invite others to join you. Do something to mark this change in your life and absorb the feeling of being the 'conqueror'.

Life is a journey. None of us are perfect and never will be. We can only strive to be the best we can be at any given time. Before moving to the next stage of your journey, celebrate that which you have already achieved.

There will always be stresses and strains in life so don't be hard on yourself if anxiety presents in a new situation in the future. Remember always what you have achieved and build on this.

Discovering you have the power to make a change and to move beyond your fears, is the basis for knowing that you always have the ability to move forward. Remain strong. Hold fast to the place of calm within you!

Authors Note:

Thank you for reading my booklet 'Seven C's to Calm – Reclaiming your anxiety-free self'.

I sincerely hope that you have gained some inspiration for your journey towards calm.

It is my intention to develop this topic with the real life case studies based on reader's experience of following this plan. The initial pilot group of readers said they found this booklet extremely useful and easy to follow.

If you are interested in providing feedback on the book you will find contact details on my website www.carolinecunningham.com or perhaps you would like to subscribe to my newsletter to be notified of additional support suggestions.

You may also like to consider my book of poetry entitled 'The Whisperings of Nature' as an accompaniment to this booklet.

'The Whisperings of Nature' is a short collection of Nature-inspired poetry offering wisdom, comfort and inspiration. It is available for on-line purchase and can be found in the book section of my website www.carolinecunningham.com

Seven C's to Calm

Work BOOK

A space for you to record some of your observations, reminders and commitments during your three month journey towards calm.

1. COMFORT

My list of comfort experiences to choose from daily/weekly:

_____

_____

_____

_____

_____

_____

Reminder: by cultivating a state of comfort and calm I will be more prepared for all outcomes.

A useful mantra for when I relax in my place of comfort:

'I am cool, calm, clear, collected'

2. COMPREHEND

Dedicating time to identifying the following:

What is anxiety?
Writing down at least two descriptions from that I have found from a dictionary and comparing this with my own description.

Anxiety Definition 1:

_____

_____

_____

Anxiety Definition 2:

_____

_____

_____

My Definition of Anxiety:

_____

_____

_____

Making a list of my anxiety symptoms?

When I am anxious, I notice the following symptoms and thoughts:

_____

_____

_____

_____

_____

_____

Do I have these symptoms all the time or only in certain situations?

I feel most anxious/tense in these situations:

_____

_____

_____

I feel slightly anxious in these situations:

_____

_____

_____

I remain gentle in my observations.

Is there a common theme to my anxiety? What is the main fixation of my anxiety or the situation in which I feel most impacted?

This is what I notice about my anxiety pattern:

_____

_____

_____

_____

_____

Taking time to research the physiological processes that are at play inside my body when anxiety is at large.

What hormones are associated with the 'fight or flight' anxiety reaction?

_____

_____

How do poor circulation and/or shallow breathing affect the nourishment of the cells in my entire body?

_____

_____

What effect does this 'extra work' of being tense and anxious have on my body's energy level or sleep pattern or the ability to think clearly?

_____

_____

To help with this task, check for articles in the book section of www.carolinecunningham.com in the book blog area.

3. CHALLENGE

Reminder:

My presence in this world is as important and necessary as that of any other living being.

In my place of comfort I remember this is so and I am open to receiving that acknowledgment in my heart.

Yes or No Answers to the following questions:

- Am I ready to make a difference to how I experience life?
- Do I prefer things as they are?
- Do I want to make a positive change?
- Am I still curious about this journey to a calmer version of myself?

Assuming those are yes answers..... Let's go! (:

Note: seek additional professional support if things are just too over-whelming! Change is possible.

4. COMMIT

My three month plan!

For starters, picking just one of my anxiety symptoms and a situation in which I feel most tense.

Allocating a score from 1 to 5 as to the intensity with which I have experienced discomfort in most recent times.

For example: 1 representing barely noticeable symptoms and 5 being the most intensely I have ever experienced anxiety symptoms.

Anxiety Symptom:

_____

Intensity 1- 5: _____

My goal:

At the end of three months I would like

to experience

_____

_____

_____

_____

This is my daily plan to restore calm:

_____

_____

_____

_____

_____

_____

_____

_____

_____

_____

_____

_____

_____

_____

_____

_____

This is my weekly plan to restore anxiety:

_____

_____

_____

_____

_____

_____

_____

_____

_____

_____

_____

Reminder:

It's not about overcoming an obstacle. Instead, I'm thinking about how much calm I want to experience.

I hold on to the feeling of calm, I relish it and make it real!

5. CHECK-IN

I check-in regularly throughout my day, making a mental note of how I feel. At the end of each day and week, I reflect on, or make note of, times when I felt good.

Referring back to my anxiety symptoms at the start, I check if the intensity of my symptoms has changed.

I revise my score at the end of each week.

If I feel I did not make much progress, I check how often I implemented my daily plan and how often I took time for comfort.

I check if there something I can improve or change for the next day or week?

I decide if this is working or if I may need extra support to get to the next stage?

Making a list of the following:

Things I am most grateful for:

_____

_____

_____

_____

_____

_____

_____

My achievements that I am most proud of:

_____

_____

_____

_____

_____

_____

_____

_____

6. CONQUER

Thinking of the word 'conquer' and thinking of the energy I associate with that word. Does it feel powerful? Is there a sense of action attached to this word?

Drawing a little picture of how I perceive the feeling of 'conquering' or winning.

These are my heroes?

_____

_____

_____

_____

_____

_____

Feeling the energy that I associate with conquering and achievement. I attempt to describe that feeling:

_____

_____

_____

_____

_____

_____

_____

7. CELEBRATE

I congratulate myself on completing this challenge!

This is what I have achieved at the end of my three month journey towards calm:

_____

_____

_____

_____

_____

_____

These are my plans for celebrating my achievement:

_____

_____

_____

_____

_____

Final reminder from the author:

There will always be stresses and strains in life so don't be hard on yourself if anxiety presents in a new situation in the future.

Remember always what you have achieved and build on this.

Discovering that you have the power to make a change and to move beyond your fears, is the basis for knowing that you always have the ability to move forward.

Remain strong!

Hold fast to the place of calm within you!

Reading Resources:

1. When Panic Attacks by Dr Áine Tubridy
2. Helping Young People Manage Anxiety by Carol Fitzpatrick
3. The Anxiety & Phobia Workbook by Edmund J. Bourne
4. The Physiology of Behaviour by Neil R. Carlson

Illustrations

*Credit: A big thank you for editorial support goes to
Marella O'Sullivan, Digital Consultant, UK/Ireland*

Cover photograph & cover design by Caroline Cunningham

Author Caroline Cunningham (Peru)